THE
PEARL
OF GREAT
PRICE

THE
PEARL
OF GREAT
PRICE

Re-discovering America's Godly Heritage

John David Matthews

Pleasant Word

Packaged by Pleasant Word, PO Box 428, Enumclaw, WA 98022. The views expressed or implied in this work do not necessarily reflect those of Pleasant Word. The author(s) is ultimately responsible for the design, content and editorial accuracy of this work.

ISBN 1-4141-0080-9
Library of Congress Catalog Card Number: 2003114735

"When the merchant found one (a pearl) of great value, he went away and sold everything he had and bought it . . ."

—Matthew 13:45

America's Godly heritage is our "pearl of great price," but it is lost to us. What would we as a nation be willing to do to get it back again?

—JDM

Dedication

This book is dedicated to my junior high history teacher, Richard Escalante, of Edwards, California, who kindled my desire to search for the truth concerning America's past.

—John David Matthews

Table of Contents

Foreword

$\mathcal{M}$any people have asked me why I would write this book with so many books like it appearing on the literary scene. If you are like me, then you have grown weary of the gross disinformation and historical revisionism that constantly flows out of the media and other people who promote an anti-American agenda in this country. For example, Public Broadcasting System (PBS) ran an interview with a prominent history professor from Lehigh University recently. This professor claimed that the event of Washington praying at Valley Forge never really occurred. Most of us have seen the beautiful painting of Washington kneeling in prayer at Valley Forge by the famous artist Arnold Friberg. Recently, I have discovered documentation in the form of irrefutable testimony and witness to Washington's act of praying in a spruce grove at Valley Forge. Since the witness to Washington's act of prayer was none other than his landlord, Isaac Potts, who was himself a devout Quaker and pacifist, it is highly probably that the event did occur. And since the honorable professor from Lehigh has absolutely no tangible evidence to prove otherwise, we must believe the evidence that is available to us.

The point is that there are dozens of incidences of disinformation and revisionism occurring every day in our schools and social and political institutions all across our country. It is up to you and me to point out the truth concerning our Godly forefathers to an unbelieving nation whenever possible. Jesus tells us that true slavery comes upon us when we begin to believe lies and untruth: "Whoever lives by the truth comes into the light" (John 3:21) and: "It is the truth that shall set you free" (John 8:32). My hope is that you will join me in the struggle to lead our fellow Americans to the truth concerning our nation's Godly heritage.

J.D.M.

CHAPTER ONE

Conflict of Ideologies

For the past four decades, America has been plagued with the actions of historical revisionists invading our cultural, intellectual, and historical institutions. The problem in accepting historical revisionism without question is two-fold: not only are we then linked to a false past based on incorrect facts, we are also denied the privilege of learning from our past mistakes. As a result of this revisionism, our public school systems continue to teach our children the untrue and misguided idea that our system of democracy has evolved without the influence of America's religious institutions. In the same manner that evolution is taught as a scientific fact instead of the postulation and mere theory that it really is, America's children are taught that our democratic system of government came about simply by "random chance." Little, if anything, is ever mentioned concerning the Christian influence that the original Puritan settlers and our Founding Fathers contributed spiritually to our governmental and social institutions. Regardless of the abundance of documented proof, the liberal and humanistic elements of our society insist on promoting the concepts that our Founding Fathers were all atheists, drunkards, and political and social opportunists. The governmental and historical record that establishes our forefathers as Godly and principled men is being systematically removed from our nation's history books and our public consciousness. Why? The answer is: to impose secular and modernist thinking upon the American populace. By removing all aspects of religious influence from public life, the Liberal and Modernist movements hope to dismantle the traditional values system that has served America in good stead for nearly 250 years. The focus of this "intellectual cleansing" is in the American judicial system. If the interpretation of the original intent concerning the doctrine of the separation of church and state can continue to be distorted as it has been since 1949, then the Liberal and Modernist movements can impose their values on our society. In this book, I hope to re-establish some of the historical truths of Christian influence from our history, and demonstrate the immense value that those influences had upon our society. Consider the words of John Adams, our second President and signer of the Declaration of Independence: "Our Constitution was made only for a moral and religious people . . . it is totally inadequate for the government of any other."[1] To subtract all Christian values and influences from our history distorts that history to the point that it literally has no meaning to us and to future generations.

CHAPTER TWO

The Great Awakening

THE PIVOTAL EVENT OF AMERICAN HISTORY

Christian influence on our society truly began at the point of our nation's colonization. The Puritans that fled religious persecution in England and settled in Holland in 1609 eventually established the Massachusetts Bay Colony in 1620. They were followed to America by the Brethren, or the German Baptists, that also fled persecution in Germany and settled in eastern Pennsylvania. No less than 22 different Christian sects settled on the eastern seaboard of America between the years 1620–1700. It was this majority of Christians that would make conditions conducive for the event of the Great Awakening, or

17

great Christian revival that would begin in America in 1734.

There is little doubt that the event of the Great Awakening was the single most significant event to influence the American Revolution. Sadly, our recorded history does not even recognize the Great Awakening as being even a minor factor in the social changes that led to the American Revolution. But the fact remains that without the great revival of 1734, Americans never would have been conscious of their desire for religious and social freedom. President Calvin Coolidge explained the true significance of the Great Awakening as a watershed event in American history:

> "The American Revolution was preceded by the Great Awakening . . . the religious revival that swept America in the middle of the 18th century. When common people began to diligently study the Bible . . . when they were stirred to a great revival, the way was prepared. The Christian religion gave the American people a new importance and a new glory, and in turn, the people demanded a new freedom and a new government. If the institutions that the Founding Fathers adopted are to survive, it will be because our people continue to have similar religious beliefs. It is useless to discuss freedom and equality in any other context. This is why the law it-

self is so *impotent*. To make or cancel laws is really not progress in itself . . . change must occur in each individual heart. The law itself cannot make men righteous. There will be a proper use of our material prosperity when and only when the individual feels a divine responsibility towards God. There will be a true obedience to the law when the individual feels that his government represents the *divine authority* of God. It is these religious convictions that represent the strength of America . . . for it is righteousness that exaults a nation."[1]

The Great Awakening was a general revival of Evangelical Christianity in the American colonies that reached its peak in the early 1740s. Prior to this, local revivals had occurred, inspired by the teachings of such clergymen as Jonathan Edwards and George Whitefield. These outdoor gatherings drew such large crowds that they caused the local revivals to merge into one "Great Awakening."

The Great Awakening had a conservative effect on all of America. During the period between 1735–1745, the majority of the American citizenry devoted their time in the pursuit of God. The main activities of many New England towns, whether day or night, was the reading and the reciting of the scriptures. Churches and public meeting halls were constantly filled with worshippers and seekers.

Some evangelists held continuous revival services all day and most of the evening. This tremendous focus on God had a profound effect on the consciousness of the American people. The revival drew fellow countrymen together, producing a sense of unity that transcended denominational, political and social boundaries. A new system of values came into being in the American heart. It was reasoned by the people that if God placed such a great value on the individual, as Christ did when He sacrificed Himself for the whole of mankind, then the true value of an individual should include the freedom from slavery in all forms. As a result of the Awakening, a yearning for religious, political and social freedom took root in the American heart. Not only did the desire for religious freedom begin to grow, but the virtues of thrift and hard work were also a product of their intense study of God's word. The desire to participate in a system of free enterprise was another product of the biblical concept of self-worth through Christ. Hence, the Great Awakening was responsible for the additional resentment that developed among the colonists towards the heavy burdens of taxation and regulation imposed upon them by Great Britain.

By the advent of the 18th century, America became a people focused on the concepts of true Chris-

tianity and true religious, social and political freedom. As President Coolidge said: "America was born
in a great revival of Christianity."[2]

GEORGE WHITEFIELD'S ROLE IN THE GREAT AWAKENING

The zenith of the Great Awakening occurred when
George Whitefield, the great English evangelist, began his first mission to the American colonies in
1739. Whitefield had already established an orphanage through his church at Bethesda, Georgia. Much
of the money raised through offerings given during
Whitefield's revival tours went to his orphanage
work. The word began to spread that Whitefield had
begun a series of revival meetings along the Atlan-
tic coast. Newspapermen such as Benjamin Franklin,
began reporting on Whitefield's sermons and writings and many people travelled from state to state
just to take part in one of Whitefield's "Holy Ghost"
revivals. When Whitefield and Franklin finally met
in Franklin's hometown of Philadelphia, a friendship began between the two men that would greatly
influence the thinking of Americans. Benjamin
Franklin became an American patriot who was
greatly influenced by the ideas of George Whitefield.

Franklin recorded his observations of the
Great Awakening during the years from 1740–

1745. Speaking specifically about Whitefield's revival services, Franklin remarked: "He (Whitefield) was at first permitted to preach in some of the churches, but the clergy soon took a dislike to him. They refused him their pulpits, so he took to preaching in the fields. The multitudes of all sects and denominations that attended outdoor sermons was enormous."[3]

Franklin then commented on the profound changes that he observed in the people attending the revivals: "It was wonderful to see the change soon made in the manners of our inhabitants. Far from being thoughtless or indifferent concerning religion, it seemed as if all the world was growing religious, so that one could not walk through any town without hearing Psalms sung by different families on every street."

Even though America was sparsely populated compared to Great Britain, phenomenally large crowds were attending Whitefield's revivals. For example, the population of Boston during this time was between 10,000 and 12,000 people. But more than 15,000 people attended Whitefield's revival at the Boston Commons. So, what was happening? The Spirit of God was moving the American citizenry to follow Whitefield's revival schedule so that their personal revival experience would continue. For example, the revival in the Boston area continued for a year and a half after Whitefield moved on, with more than 30 new churches taking root as a result of Whitefield's revival meetings. Worship services were occurring daily, and not just in churches, but in business buildings and private homes.[4] The Holy Spirit of God was moving in a powerful way wherever Whitefield preached.

In 1741, Whitefield left America for England, but his impact on the Great Awakening in the American colonies had been incredible. Through Whitefield's meetings, the Congregational churches of the northern and mid-Atlantic states, specifically the Baptist and Presbyterian denominations, had been dynamically rekindled. Whitefield would return to America again in 1754 for another year long revival tour, and then return again briefly in the years 1763 and 1768. These later visits had the effect of sustaining the intensity of the Great Awakening up to the years just prior to the Revolutionary War. There is little doubt that the movement of the Holy Spirit upon the American people had the effect of beginning an intense desire for religious and social freedom . . . and George Whitefield played a huge role in the development of America's spiritual heritage.

THE IMPORTANCE OF THE GREAT AWAKENING

Undoubtedly, the greatest single event in American history up to the event of the Revolutionary War was George Whitefield's series of revivals in the American colonies from 1739–1770 that were known in history as the "Great Awakening." I don't know about you, but my history books in grade and high school never mentioned the event of the Great Awakening. But when this little known event is factored into its proper place in early American history, one realizes the importance that this revival had in changing the hearts and minds of the American colonists concerning their manifest destiny. The fact is that without a movement of the Holy Spirit upon the American people at this time, there would have never been a call to revolution. Whitefield's last visit to America was in 1770, just three months after the event of the Boston Massacre. Whitefield was well appraised of what the political climate was in the American colonies . . . and although he was a British citizen, Whitefield was well aware of the fact that as men drew closer to God, their desire for social, political and economic freedom always grew stronger.

The revival fires caused by the event of the Great Awakening galvanized the American colonists into a single people . . . a people who believed that they were called by God to participate in a divine mission. Through revival, God revealed to the American people not only the nature of that mission, which was to establish a nation based on man's relationship to God and the freedoms and benefits that resulted from that relationship. God not only revealed the nature of His mission in establishing this new nation, He also picked the men who would lead America through the turmoil of the war and beyond, establishing a form of government based on biblical principles. But there can be no doubt that the catalyst that started the Revolutionary War was the event of the Great Awakening, begun by John and Charles Wesley and George Whitefield in England and brought to America by the divine direction of God.

CHAPTER THREE

The Religious Origins of our Democracy

ur Founding Fathers have left us a written legacy of our Christian heritage that we can trace back through the years of our country's history. That legacy can be discovered both in the official documentation of the institutions of our government, and in the documentation of the private lives of our nation's leaders. President John Adams made this comment while addressing Congress: "The general principles on which our forefathers achieved independence were the principles of Christianity. I believe that these principles of Christianity are as eternal as the existence of God."[1]

President John Quincy Adams once asked, "Why is it that the Fourth of July and Christmas are the two most important holidays in America?" President Adams answered his own question: "The birthday of the nation is linked to the birth of Christ because our nation was founded on the precepts of Christianity and the teachings of Jesus." President Adams also said, "The greatest victory won in the American Revolution was that Christian principles and civil government would be united together in an *absolute* and *insoluble* bond." The first Chief Justice of the Supreme Court and one of the primary authors of the Constitution, John Jay, wrote, "It is the duty of our Christian nation to elect Christians as our leaders." [1]

In his farewell address to the nation, George Washington focused on how our nation's prosperity was directly linked to the degree of religion and morality that was currently in existence in our nation. He said: "No one can be called an American patriot if they attempt to separate our political structure from Christianity. If you attempt to separate religion and morality from government, you cannot be a true American patriot."[3]

These statements by some of our most prominent Founding Fathers are well documented by public and private record. Where did our Founding Fathers get their ideas for establishing a government based on Christian principles? In a University of Houston study done nearly 20 years ago, the researchers documented exactly 3,154 direct quotes made by our Founding Fathers during the Revolutionary War years, and traced all of the sources of their quotes. They found that:

> Baron Charles Montescu, a Christian, was quoted 8.3% of the time, or 252 times, Sir William Blackstone, a Christian lawyer, was quoted 7.9% of the time, or 242 times, John Locke, a Christian philosopher and teacher, was quoted 2.9% of the time, or 94 times.

But the Bible was quoted by the Founding Fathers *four* times more than these three top scholars combined![4] Thirty-four percent of all of the Founding Fathers' recorded quotations came directly from the Bible. And interestingly enough, Blackstone's famous commentaries on the law had only one source—the Bible, which was his source for developing legal statutes patterned after the Levitical law and the Laws of Moses set forth in the first five books of the Bible, the Pentateuch. As America's legal system developed, its primary source material came from two primary sources—Blackstone's English Law Dictionary and the Holy Bible! So historically, we can establish without a doubt that the Founding Fathers were under a dynamic and powerful Christian influence at the time of the birth of our nation.

SOME SOURCES OF CHRISTIAN INFLUENCE IN EARLY AMERICAN SOCIETY

What were some of the societal institutions that were transformed by Christian influence in early America? We see Christian values permeating pre-Revolutionary War America at a time when the rest of the world was struggling in a moral and social vacuum. But at this time, America had already established institutions which caused the development of a moral and spiritual fiber in the fabric of its society. Some of these were:

EDUCATION

The Christian-based educational system of pre-Revolutionary War America produced the New England Primer, the first mass-produced school textbook in North America in 1690. This was a first grade reader that was based on Bible verse and fact. Children were taught to read, write and reason using God's word. This educational primer became a standard school text in the colonies until the end of the 19th century. The New England Primer was the forerunner of the popular McGuffey Reader, which also contained many biblical references and values. The McGuffey Reader would become the most widely used textbook in U.S. history. Up to the end of World

War I, 1918, the two most commonly used textbooks in the American school system were the McGuffey Reader and the Bible.[5]

PUBLIC OPINION

One of the earliest institutions used to disseminate personal opinion was the Christian publishing organization known as the American Tract Society. The American Tract Society is still in operation today, but it began publishing religious tracts or pamphlets in the early 1700s in the American colonies. The authors of these tracts published by the society before and during the Revolution was a "who's who" of the Founding Fathers and the signers of the Declaration of Independence. Over half of the Declaration's signers were writers for the Tract Society. These tracts were the modern day equivalent of today's newspapers and other mass media writings. Because of the scarcity of books, these tracts were the only source available for the printed word, along with newspapers during that early period. Therefore, they had a tremendous influence on American thought and opinion. The most well-known tract published before the Revolution was Thomas Paine's "Common Sense," but many other tracts written by America's religious and political leadership were just as influential.

POLITICS

The important events of early American history were recorded in documents that were later published as pamphlets, tracts, and even books. These recorded events were published with the intent of being used to educate and opinionate the American people. For example, George Washington's farewell address as he left the presidency was published and used as a grade school textbook from the early to the middle 1800s. It was promoted by the educational system at that time as being the greatest example of public speaking ever given in U.S. history. In his address, Washington gave the nation two foundations which he thought would insure the nation's prosperity in the future: the foundations of religion and morality.[2] Without these two foundations, Washington said, our nation would fail as an institution of freedom and opportunity for all of mankind. In his departing words, Washington went on to say that no one could be considered an American patriot if he tried to separate religion and morality from government and public life. In hearing this, one wonders if today's liberal politicians of the likes of Ted Kennedy, Joe Biden, Pat Leahy, and Barney Franks would initiate impeachment hearings against Washington if he were president today.

By the beginning of World War I, the book of Washington's farewell address had all but vanished from the nation's libraries and bookstores. But there was no doubt that it was one of the most influential writings to affect American thought in the first 150 years of American history.

CHAPTER FOUR

Historical Revisionism

The corporate mission that was divinely given to those Christian men and women who first came to America was this: that in great need and humility, a small body of Christians would put themselves in the hands of their Sovereign Lord and commit their lives both to God and to one another. One would only have to read the contents of the Mayflower Compact to realize that this dual horizontal and vertical commitment was a reality in the lives of the Puritan settlers of New England. The pledge that each man on the Mayflower signed read like this:

"In the name of God, Amen. We whose names are under written, having undertaken, for the glory of God and the advancement of the Christian faith, a voyage to plant the first colony in the northern parts of Virginia, do by these present do solemnly and mutually in the presence of God and one another, covenant and combine ourselves together into a civic body politic, for our better ordering and preservation and furtherance of the ends foresaid, and by the virtue hereof to enact, constitute and frame such just and equal laws, as shall be thought most meet and convenient for the general good of the colony. Unto which we promise all due submission and obedience. In witness thereof, we have hereunder subscribed our names . . ."[1]

This idea of a dual commitment to God and fellow man was the blueprint of the settling of early America up to the time and beyond the event of the Revolutionary War. Thomas Paine wrote in his "Call for Independance" in 1776: "We have every opportunity to form the noblest, purest constitution on the face of the earth. We have it in our power to begin the world over again. A situation similar to the present has not happened since the days of Noah, until now . . . the birthday of a New World is at hand."[2] How then, did the historical revisionists of the 20th century possibly come to be so wrong concerning the motivations and the values of our Founding Fathers, when the historical record gives undeniable proof as to what those motivations and values were? Let us now look at some of the popular historical revisions of our nation's early history that appear in many of the most used American history textbooks found in our nation's school systems.

MYTH NUMBER ONE

The explorers and early settlers of America were completely profit-motivated. They were either after gold, a new trade route to China and the Indies, or a shorter route to resources for the slave trade.

So many current history textbooks stress obsessive greed as the prime motivation of the early explorers and settlers of America. But one needs only to closely research the historical record in order to discover the true motivation of those early pioneers. Christopher Columbus said: "It was the Lord who put into my mind the fact that it would be possible to sail from here to the Indies . . . I could feel His hand upon me . . . there is no question that the inspiration was from the Holy Spirit, because he comforted me with rays of inspiration from the Holy Scriptures."[3] Columbus continues: "I am a most unworthy sinner, but I have cried out to the Lord for grace and mercy, and He has covered me completely. For the execution of my journey to the Indies, I did not make use of intelligence, mathematics or maps . . . it is simply the fulfillment of what Isaiah had prophesied. No one should fear to undertake any task in the name of Our Savior, if the goal is just and the intention is purely for His Holy Service. The working out of all things has been assigned to each person by our Lord."[4] Columbus would later say: "O, what a gracious Lord, who desires that people should perform for Him those things for which He holds Himself responsible! Day and night, moment by moment, everyone should express their most devoted gratitude to Him."[4] Just think! The discoverer of the Americas actually gloried in the fact that his accomplishments were divinely inspired and directed by God! Have you ever even heard or seen these quotes in any grade school, junior high, or high school American history book? You won't, because the concept of trusting in God is completely foreign to 20th Century thinking.

In Cotton Mather's "History of New England" (1730), John Higginson, who wrote the preface for Mather's book, said: "One of the great and wonderful works of God was that He stirred up the spirits of so many thousands of His servants, to transport themselves to the wilderness of America, for the purpose of a fuller and better Reformation of the Church of God than had yet appeared in the world"[5]. Higginson voiced the purpose and plan that the early settlers of New England believed they were carrying out: "The new settlers saw themselves individually and corporately in the state of a continuing need of God's forgiveness, mercy, and support."[6] So, by recorded history, we see that the corporate mission divinely given to those Christian men and women who came to America in order to practice religious freedom was this: that in great need and humility, a small body of Christians would put themselves in the hands of their Lord and commit their lives to one another . . . hence the blueprint for living in the early Puritan colonies of North America.

MYTH NUMBER TWO

The Founding Fathers were not religious men, but were atheists and deists.

This seems to be the most controversial topic concerning historical revisionism today. I find myself in a constant debate with an endless line of secular journalists and pseudo-historians who are totally ignorant of America's true history and heritage. Why do these people insist that America's early leaders could not have been men of faith? I believe that the answer to this question is that these people see the moral and spiritual decline in America today and they simply cannot believe that it could have been any different here 250 years ago. Then there is the condition that psychologists call "self-projection" .

. . these historical revisionists are eager to portray our Founding Fathers as without principles and morally and spiritually bankrupt because that is the exact condition of their own hearts. Again, to discover the truth about the true spiritual and moral character of our nation's early leaders, we simply have to study the original, unedited literature and documentation that they have left us. In the most desperate hour of the American Revolution, our leaders signed a document that above and beyond all else confirmed their faith and trust in the God of Abraham, Isaac and Jacob: "We hold these truths to be self evident . . . that all men are created equal . . . and they are endowed by their creator with certain unalienable rights." Because they placed their full trust and faith in this God, they claimed the very gifts that they knew that their God had given them by the promise of His written word. And those gifts were, "Life, liberty, and the pursuit of happiness."

Benjamin Franklin, one of the most intellectual of the Founding Fathers, made this fantastic statement, expressing the feeling of the majority of Revolutionary War America.

> "In the beginning of this conflict with Britain, we (the congress) had daily prayers in this room (the halls of congress in Philadelphia) for divine protection. Our prayers were heard, and they were graciously answered. All of us who were

engaged in this struggle must have observed frequent instances of *supernatural providence* in our favor. And have we now forgotten this powerful friend? Or do we imagine that we no longer need His assistance? I have lived, sir, a long time, and the longer that I live, the more convinced I am of this truth: That God governs the affairs of men . . . and, If a sparrow cannot fall to the ground without His notice, is it possible that an empire can rise without His aid?"[7]

George Washington, the father of our nation in both the military and political struggle that the country faced, was unquestionably a man of great faith. In the book "George Washington the Christian," there is a section of Washington's personal prayers. One of these prayers, "The Daily Sacrifice," we see that Washington was a man of great devotion and faith towards God. This beautiful personal prayer shows us Washington's personal relationship with God:

"O most glorious God, I acknowledge and confess my faults, in the weak and imperfect performance of my duties of this day, I have called upon you for pardon and forgiveness of my sins . . . but so coldly and carelessly do I approach you that my prayers have become my sin, and I stand in the need of your pardon. I have heard your

Holy Word, but with such deafness of spirit that I have been an unprofitable and forgetfull hearer. But, O God, thou art rich in mercy and plenteous in redemption . . . mark not, I beseech thee, what I have done amiss! Remember that I am but dust, and remit my transgressions and cover them all with the absolute obedience of your dear Son . . . that those sacrifices of sin, praise, and thanksgiving which I have offered may be accepted by You, in and for the sacrifice of Jesus Christ offered upon the cross for me."[8]

The powerful humility and repentant attitude that Washington offers to God in this prayer speaks volumes to us of his relationship with his God. We can see how Washington was sustained by his faith in such terrible times of hardship by the power and sincerity of his prayers. These are just some of the gems that we have in the treasure of our Christian heritage, that is documented for us in our historical archives. All one needs to do is spend some time seeking out the Christian heritage that is recorded in our nation's history.

CHAPTER FIVE

Christianity's Influence on American Government

$\mathcal{U}$p to the event of World War I, both Congress and the Supreme Court had repeatedly given its approval to the value of Christianity in American public life. In 1853, a political group petitioned Congress to begin to implement a plan that would in essence separate the church from all forms of public life. As a result of this action, both branches of Congress conducted studies on the feasibility of actually separating religion from politics in our governmental system. Both the Senate and the House findings were placed in a report to the full U.S. Congress in 1854 . . . their summation said this:

"Had the Founding Fathers had any suspicion of an attempt to eradicate Christianity during the Revolution, that Revolution would have been strangled in its cradle. At the time of the adoption of the Constitution, the universal sentiment was that Christianity should be encouraged, but let not any one sect of that religion be dominant."[1]

Nearly a century after the American Revolution, we still had political leaders that saw the value of integrating politics with the Christian religion. And, the Judiciary Committee statement proves that those leaders still understood Jefferson's original intent of the "wall of separation" . . . that it referred to only the doctrine of non-denominational dominance by any specific sect of the Christian religion. The Christian religion was welcomed with open arms to enter the arena of politics and public life in America.

Two months later, in that same year of 1854, the same combined Judiciary Committee from the two houses of Congress, issued a secondary report which further clarified the government's position on the relationship between church and state . . . it said: "The great single element in our political system is the belief of our people in the pure doctrines and the divine truths of the Gospel of Jesus Christ."[2] Whew!! What I would not give for the opportunity to read this statement by that Judiciary Committee of 1854 to every one of the current Justices of the Supreme Court! The incredible thing is that that same Judiciary Committee of 1854 cited the letter from Jefferson to the Danbury church as its prime source of *prior documentation*!! The fact is that most congressional and judicial scholars, constitutional lawyers, and even federal and supreme court justices are ignorant of the fact that the Jefferson letter is on record in legal ruling after legal ruling as the prime constitutional document favoring the integration of church and state!!

John Jay was the first Chief Justice of the United States Supreme Court. History tells us that between he, James Madison, and Thomas Jefferson, no three other men were more responsible for the conception and writing of the Constitution. John Jay, with the aid of James Madison, co-authored a series of articles printed in the Federalist Papers that were to be a commentary on the articles of the Constitution. In the first series of articles, Jay said: "The primary political motive of man is self-interest. Man is by nature selfish, and at best, imperfectly rational. It is only by the guidance and influence of God that man can achieve anything of lasting value."[3] No wonder the Founding Fathers sought to keep religion in America's public life. Here, John Jay, the chief interpreter of our nation's laws and one of the chief architects of our nation's governing documents, emphasizes the essential nature and reason for involving the Christian religion into our nation's political system. One wonders what the opinion of the current group of Supreme Court justices would be after they had read Justice Jay's comments in these Federalist Papers! But John Jay went beyond the advocation of merely combining religious principles with the mechanics of American government. In a later ruling, Justice Jay also said: "Providence has given us the privilege to choose our leaders . . . therefore, it is our duty to select Christians as our rulers."[4]

The Founding Fathers knew the value of having faith in God in its struggle to become a nation. That is why they continually sought men of God to continue the building of a government which combined public life with Christianity . . . in short they strove to continue the concept of . . . "One Nation Under God."

CHAPTER SIX

The Separation of Church and State

AN ABERRATION IN AMERICAN HISTORY

*I*f one has ever made an extensive study of the American legal system, one will discover that our laws have been developed and implemented through two basic test conditions: *original intent* and *legal precedents*. And if one has ever studied the history and circumstances surrounding the now-famous Jefferson letter to the Danbury Baptist Church of Danbury, Connecticut, it is easy to see that there were the grossest of errors made by America's legal system in interpreting Jefferson's *original intent*. For both the conditions of *original intent* and *legal precedent* were both ignored in the

1949 Supreme Court ruling on separatioan of church and state.

The facts concerning the incident of Jefferson responding to a letter written by a woman from the congregation of the Danbury Baptist Church are as follows; The woman, who wrote Jefferson on November 17, 1801, had a concern over the freedom to freely worship in lieu of the supposed authority of the federal government's ability to regulate the practice of religion. In his response, Jefferson said that the woman's concerns were unfounded, for according to the First Amendment to the Constitution, there was a "wall of separation" between church and state that protected all forms of religion from being regulated and even limited or abolished by the federal government. We know this to be the correct interpretation of Jefferson's famous response because of the historic *legal precedence* that is on record in our judicial system. For example, in 1853, a group of Rationalists concerned with the pervasion of religion into the military, petitioned Congress to eliminate the position of chaplain throughout the military. As a response, in a congressional report from both houses of the U.S. Congress, the legislative branch of our government collectively said:

In this age, there is no substitute for Christianity . . . it was the religion of our Founding Fathers, and they expected it to remain the religion of their descendants. The very thing that holds our governmental system together is the belief in the pure doctrines and the divine truths of Jesus Christ."[1]

The Supreme Court agreed and summarily dismissed the case against the military chaplaincy service.

Through their rulings, the Supreme Court also established a direct connection between the country's moral standards and the teaching of Christianity. In 1844, a school in Philadelphia decided that they would completely eliminate the teachings of Christianity from their curriculum, stating that they could teach morality to their students without the aid of Christian doctrine. The national outrage against the school was so intense that the case was quickly forced into the Supreme Court. In its commentary on their ruling, the court said: "Why may not the Bible, and especially the New Testament be read and taught as a *divine revelation* in our schools? . . . it's general precepts expounded and its glorious principles of morality taught . . . where can the purest principles of morality be learned so clearly or so perfectly than from the New Testament of the Bible?"[2]

THE PERVERSION OF JEFFERSON'S DOCTRINE

The Jefferson doctrine found in the Danbury letter was completely consistent with Jefferson's contributions to the First Amendment to the Constitution. In it, Jefferson stated: "Congress shall not make one religion *meritorious* over another, or establish a state religion." Jefferson further stated that the freedom of religion was a God-given or *inalienable* right, and therefore could never be controlled or regulated by the federal government. In his exposition on the First Amendment in the "Federalist Papers," Jefferson again stated: "There should be a wall of separation between church and state in regard to the *regulation* of religion, to insure that the government would never interfere with *any religious activity*."

Probably the greatest legal mystery in American history is how the Supreme Court was able to misinterpret Jefferson's letter to the Danbury church in lieu of his writing of the First Amendment to the Constitution and his complete exposition on the subject of religious freedom in the "Federalist Papers." Jefferson's original intent was so clear that it could be understood by the simplest and most elemental of minds. As a brief experiment, I read the Danbury letter to my 12-year old daughter, and then I asked her to explain the letter to me. This she was able to do in the simplest of terms. One wonders how the supposed greatest of legal minds in our nation back in 1949 could have grossly misinterpreted such a simple, basic document.

As we have said, the historical turning point in the Supreme Court's position concerning the compatibility of religion and government occurred in 1949. Up to this point, the Supreme Court had ruled in favor of religion being an integral part of American life no less than 85 times in the court's history! But in 1949, while ruling in the case of Everson vs. the State Board of Education, the Supreme Court finally took the Jefferson letter completely out of context by using only nine words from the entire text. The court said that the First Amendment had: "Erected a wall of separation between church and state"[3], and that wall had to be kept high and impregnable. By ruling against the board of education, which had desired to continue Christian teaching in the school system, the Supreme Court commented: "This is what the Founding Fathers originally intended . . . a separation of church and state . . . this was their great intent."[4] So the grand mystery of our age is: how can a supposedly learned and educated group of men versed in American law and case history make such a gross error concerning *original intent* and *legal precedence*? By closely examining the members of that 1949 Supreme Court, we can see how such a gross misinterpretation could be possible.

CHAPTER SEVEN

The Infamous 1949 Supreme Court

There were two definitive factors that influenced the 1949 Supreme Court's decision concerning "Everson vs. The Board of Education." The most evident factor was that the 1949 court was predominantly composed of Franklin D. Roosevelt (F.D.R.) appointees. These men were all hand-picked by Roosevelt himself, and were required to pass a three-part "litmus test" of suitability. 1. Roosevelt always demanded *absolute loyalty* from his appointees. 2. Roosevelt only appointed fellow big government advocates, enabling him to practice extraordinary powers well beyond the needs of the depression and war eras. 3. Roosevelt required that his court appointees be disciples of the philosophy of *Libertarianism*.[1] The Libertarian view originated with the noble aspects of individualism and personal freedom, but by the 20th century, it evolved into a secular philosophy that believed that big government could take the place of religion in a society. Libertarians believed that man could create a moral society without God, and it was the government that could truly free mankind, that freedom coming from the socialist control of a wise and benevolent government. So, the mostly Libertarian court of 1949 wielded an anti-Christian bias and a residual "New Deal" view of what the government's function in society should be.

So, who were the members of the 1949 Supreme Court? A brief look at each member is highly revealing.

Tom C. Clark: Mr. Clark was a Truman loyalist who transformed into a supporter of big government. He was known mostly for his advocation of abolishing a proposed loyalty oath for state and federal employees. Tom Clark's worldly socialist philosophy took root into the mind of one of his offspring, **Ramsey Clark**, who became one of the most notorious social activitists to ever hold the office of Attorney General.

Harlan S. Stone: Stone was one of the oldest members of the 1949 court, being appointed by Calvin

Coolidge. He was a fellow student with Coolidge at Amhurst College. Stone became a defender of Roosevelt's New Deal, and was a constant advocate of expanding the Federal Government's power. Stone was one of the sponsors of the court's opinion in their Separation of Church and State ruling in 1949.

Hugo Black: Black is credited with creating the legal machinery that saw the government transform into a national regulatory authority. Black was the architect of the expansion of the War Powers Act. Black's greatest "black eye" during his tenure as a justice came when it was learned that he was a card-carrying member of the Ku Klux Klan (KKK), but this fact did not stop Roosevelt from nominating him to the Court. Black was continually accused by the press of racial and religious intolerance, and there were continuous impeachment efforts throughout his tenure. It was Justice Black that wrote the deciding commentary on the 1949 Separation of Church and State ruling.

Stanley F. Reed: Another F.D.R. appointee, he was an ardent New Deal supporter, and continually voted to expand the power of government. In most security and criminal justice cases, Reed sided with the government.

Felix Frankfurter: A personal friend of Roosevelt, Frankfurter was one of the few qualified members of the 1949 Court. He taught law at Harvard Law School for more than 25 years. Frankfurter was a New Deal activist who formed a Libertarian caucus with Justices Black, Douglas, Murphy and Rutledge that could not be overturned. In 1943, Frankfurter dissented on a 6–3 vote that supported a West Virginia statute that advocated the Pledge of Allegiance, and the salute to the American flag as a daily exercise. Frankfurter's dissenting opinion stated that, "the Pledge was an unconstitutional invasion of the free expression of religion." Remember, this ruling occurred in 1943, when American patriotism was at a fever pitch . . . why Justice Frankfurter was not dragged out of his courtroom and tarred and feathered is not known. But the fact remains that Justice Frankfurter had the nerve to oppose the concepts of loyalty and allegiance to the American cause at a time when that cause was in a struggle for its very existence. It is no surprise, then, that Frankfurter would pervert the traditional ideas of religion and government in the landmark court ruling of 1949, when America was at peace.

William O. Douglas: Possibly the most enigmatic and incongruent of all the members of the 1949 court. Publically, Douglas constantly preached the positive ideologies of Libertarianism . . . that the ideas and beliefs of the individual should be beyond the reach and control of the government. But his court rulings did not reflect that philosophy. For example, in 1965, Douglas ruled that birth control was a right guaranteed by the Constitution in a Connecticut state appeals case. In reality, Douglas believed that the only true freedom that man could have was the freedom that the government gave him.

Frank Murphy: Murphy was another Roosevelt appointee who advocated increasing and consolidating the government's power. Murphy was the court engineer for the development of the modern day Internal Revenue Service (IRS). One of Justice Murphy's misguided decisions was his proposal to extend the Fifth and Sixth Amendments of the Constitution to the Japanese Army Commanding General Yamashita.[2] General Yamashita was responsible for the Bataan death march in the Japanese occupation of the Philippines. Murphy's rationale was that Japan would never again become a normalized nation if America did not forgive and forget past wrongs. Needless to say, Justice Murphy was vilified by both the press and the public for his wacky suggestion.

Robert H. Jackson: Judge Jackson was unique in Supreme Court history in the fact that he had absolutely no judicial experience when Roosevelt appointed him to the court in 1941. Jackson is also known for being the chief American prosecutor in the Nuremburg War Crimes Trials. Historians will agree that his experience in Nuremburg changed his philosophy from that of a conservative interpreter of the law to a global judicial activitist. After his Nuremburg experience, Jackson began to view his concept of freedom not from an individual viewpoint, but from the stage of the world court. If Jackson now believed in subverting other foreign governments in the world arena, how did he view the rights of individuals in his own country? In 1943, Jackson voted against the use of the Pledge of Allegiance in a Carolina state appeal to his court. Jackson ruled that the state, "could not force people to act by faith, and the government could not prescribed what should be orthodox in the practice of religion."[3] Again, this decision came at a time American patriotism was at a peak . . . in the middle of World

War II. Do you think that Justice Jackson cared how he was perceived by his fellow Americans concerning his patriotism? Then why would Justice Jackson be affected by his gross misinterpretation of the First Amendment conerning religion in public life in 1949?

Fred Vinson: Judge Vinson was another Truman appointee, and possibly the most advanced Socialist in the 1949 court. His work in the Roosevelt administration included his help in the development of the T.V.A. and the National Industrial Recovery Act. Since Vinson was entirely comfortable with developing programs that expanded the power of the Federal government, he would continue to work for the expansion of governmental power in the judicial system. The extent to which Vinson would use the role of government is seen in his ruling in the Steel Seizure Case of 1952. Vinson felt that the government not only had the right to regulate the operation of American business, he felt the government should actively be involved in policy and decision making in the business sector.

There is no doubt that the combination of big government advocacy and the anti-religious bias that permeated the hearts and minds of the members of that 1949 Supreme Court was the primary cause of its infamous Everson vs. Board of Education ruling. In that ruling, the court ignored all past case law and past legal precedents in making its ruling. This, combined with the gross misinterpretation of Jefferson's original Danbury church document was the formula for what was absolutely the worst legal decision in the history of the United States Supreme Court. Remember, the two greatest elements of influence on the members of that 1949 Court were: 1) the philosophy of Libertarianism, which would later evolve into today's philosophy of Humanism. This doctrine believed that man needed no god because he was his own god. The second greatest philosophical influence on the court members was: 2) the advocacy of a strong centralized federal government that would have unlimited power. The Founding Fathers unanimously opposed a strong centralized federal government because they firmly believed that that type of government would evolve into an oppressive government that was out of control in terms of its abuse of power. The Founding Fathers were correct in their assumption that a powerful centralized government would prohibit citizens from the right to exercise their religious freedom in public life, for the 1949 court was the very instrument that an over-empowered federal government used to do just that. The results of that 1949 decision by the Supreme Court in terms of the damage it has done to the individuals and the institutions of our country is so vast and pervasive that it may never be accurately calculated!

CHAPTER EIGHT

Searching the Past for Solutions

"God looks after fools, drunks, and the United States"

—well-known saying in 1820s America

It is amazing to think that this was a well-used popular saying not more than a generation after the Revolutionary War. Even though many of the participants in that war were direct witnesses to the miracles and sustaining grace that God poured out on this country during those desperate times, the American populace began to turn their backs on God immediately after our nation's complete independence was won through the War of 1812 . . . and this condition of ungratefulness still exists today. The more that God blesses us as a nation, the more that the overt rejection of God seems to flow from the hearts and minds of most Americans. Abraham Lincoln observed this condition some 80 years after the war for independence. While giving his address marking the National Day of Fasting, Humility and Prayer in 1863, he said:

> We have been the recipients of the choicest bounties of heaven . . . we have been preserved these many years in peace and prosperity . . . we have grown in numbers, wealth and power, as no other nation has ever grown. But we have forgotten God. We have forgotten the gracious hand which preserved us in peace, and multiplied and enriched and strengthened us; and we have vainly imagined, in the deceitfulness of our hearts, that all of these blessings were produced by some superior wisdom and virtue of our own. Intoxicated with unbroken success, we have come to be too self-sufficient to feel the necessity of the redeeming and preserving grace of God . . . too proud to pray to the God that made us!"[1]

Oh, if Lincoln could only see his America today . . . would his first thought be concerned with how much of a prophet he really was in making this statement?

Recent surverys tell us that there are up to as many as 60 million evangelical Christians living in the United States. That is roughly 20% of our nation's total population. The question that we must ask ourselves is this: if these Christians are truly obeying both the Great Commandment and the Great Commission of Jesus Christ, then why are they not acting as salt and light to the rest of the nation? Many Christians here do believe that they are acting as salt and light towards others, that they are strong witnesses for the cause of Christ. But the fact is that the ills of our society have been steadily on the increase in spite of the best efforts of the church. Have we become, as Jesus said: "Salt that has lost its saltiness?" (Matt. 5:13) What is the church doing wrong today that it seems to have cancelled itself out as a leavening influence on society? Peter Marshall, the well-known author and theologian, has articulated an answer to this question: "Christian roots are shooting out rapidly in all directions in the United States . . . but what is needed is a simultaneous deepening of the **tap root**. The personal relationship that each Christian has with God must be nurtured so that it can grow and deepen, just as the tap root of a tree grows."[2] God's Word gives us the key to what each Christian must do to deepen and grow our relationship with Christ . . . 2 Chronicles 7:14 says: **"If My people who are called by My name will humble themselves and pray and seek My face . . .**

then I will hear from heaven and forgive their sin and heal their land."

In order for us to be obedient to God's call to a deeper commitment and relationship with him, we must first seek out a **model** of this relationship that we can imitate. As we mentioned earlier in this book, the pilgrims made a commitment to a deeper relationship with both God and their fellow man, and the product of that covenant relationship was the **Mayflower Compact**. To the pilgrims, a deeper relationship with God meant that their humility and obedience before God would be forever on the increase . . . and that deepening, dependent relationship with God would be reflected in the relationship that they had with the people in their communities. The increase in their dependence upon God also brought them a desire to serve and become deeply involved in the lives of other people. This dual relationship with both God and man is exactly the call to humility that God speaks of in 2 Chron. 7:14. How willing are we today to attempt to become true servants of those around us, and in turn, allow them to become involved in our own lives? According to God's plan of abundant life for His followers, our vertical relationship with God will continue to mature as our horizontal relationship with our fellow matures in a God-like fashion. The pilgrims were the closest to mimicking the early church of the first century after Christ's death, as spoken of in the Book of Acts. In chapter 4, verse 32, it says: "They (the church) shared everything they had with one another" . . . and in Acts 2:44–45, it says: "All the believers were together, and had everything in common . . . selling their possessions and goods, they gave to everyone as he had need." But let's face it . . . most of us believe in our hearts that the early church of the first century A.D. was far too radical in terms of their relationships with each other . . . after all, we live in a society based on free enterprise and individualism . . . their kind of mutually dependent relationship would not work in our society. Maybe it is true that the very structure of American society is one of the inhibiting factors when it comes to a national revival. Our forefathers, the pilgrims, knew the value of becoming one body united by their relationships with God and each other. The fact is that the answer to America's problems does not depend on a complete, heartfelt, radical change by every member of our society. According to God's promise in 2 Chronicles, it says: **"If My people . . . ."** A spiritual revival in our nation depends on whether the Christians in our nation are willing to make the effort to seek a deeper relationship with God and their fellow Christians. Can we as the followers of Christ humble ourselves to the point that our relationship with God can be renewed and rejuvenated?

Let us now scrutinize the promise that God has made to us in 2 Chronicles 7:14. What does God require of us, and what will He do if we obey Him?

"If My people who are called by My name will humble themselves and pray and seek My face and turn from their wicked ways, then I will hear from heaven, and will forgive their sin and will heal their land."

"If My people who are called by My name . . ."

God does not call all of his people to do every task that He needs to have done . . . and God does not call on all of His people to begin revival. Historically, God has always used a small number of His people to achieve great things. Remember Gideon, who had an army of many thousands, but God cut that number down to just a few hundred. Gideon used that small number of followers to defeat a huge Midianite army. Jesus turned the world around with just twelve disciples . . . God does incredible things with just a few faithful followers. **"If My people"** tells us that if just a faithful few will begin to pray for revival and renewal across our land, God will honor that attempt.

Who does God use to reflect His glory? Scripture tells us that it is those who are **"called by His name."** The names for God in the Old Testament are too many to mention . . . but there is only one name for God in the New Testament that is as well used, and that is the name "**Christ**." For Christ is God, and those that follow Christ are known as **Christians**. So we know that even in the Old Testament, God prophesied concerning who He would call on to initiate revival . . . it is through God's people who are called Christians.

". . . **will humble themselves** . . ."

One of the major problems in Christian America today is that most believers do not understand what it truly means to humble themselves before God. Most Christians believe that humbling themselves before God means that they are to show up for church on Sunday mornings and then maybe again on Sunday or Wednesday evenings. But God's word indicates that the act of humbling ourselves before God takes on a completely different meaning and requires an entirely different discipline rather than routine.

The Greek word for "humble" is the word "tapeinos," which means "to be brought low or abased." When we think of the examples of humility found in the Bible, we find no greater example of humility that Christ's redemptive act of the cross. Scripture tells us that Jesus humbled himself "by making Himself nothing for our sakes" (Phil. 2:7). It is hard for us to understand how the only Son of God was able to make Himself nothing in His humility for us, but Jesus sets a standard that every Christian is to emulate. As Christ humbled Himself for us before His Father, we must do the same in total obedience, humility and faith.

"... if My people will pray ..."

Part of the humility that God requires of us is the re-establishment of our communication with Him. God wants us to have a personal, intimate level of communication with Him through our prayer life. The main activity in the lives of our pilgrim forefathers was a constant daily routine of corporate and private prayer. I am fortunate to own a copy of the Congressional record, recorded from the time of the American Revolution up to the beginning of the 19th century. And in that record are numerous references of the Continental Congress breaking from the business at hand to spend time together in prayer. Also a matter of public record is Washington's fervent prayers for deliverance while he was at Valley Forge. Washington's landlord, Isaac Potts, was a witness to one of these prayer sessions by Washington. Potts had this to say about Washington's prayers: "If George Washington be not a man of God, then I am greatly deceived . . . and still shall I be more deceived if God does not, through him, work out a great salvation for America."

The painting of the Continental Congress in prayer done by the well-known artist Benjamin West, at one time hung in the lobby of Congress. But now, it has been relegated to a storage area in the basement of that same building. We as a nation have completely abandoned the effort of praying together as a united people . . . we have forgotten how God has used our nation's prayers in the past to deliver us through incredible adversities and trials. But God's promise to us as a nation is still that if we would turn to Him in a corporate movement by humbling ourselves before Him in prayer, then He would pour out His unlimited blessings on us.

". . . and seek My face . . ."

The Greek translation for the phrase "seek My face" or "zealousy seek" is the phrase "zeloo orego." When God asks us to seek His face, He calls on us to a complete work. He calls us to desire to be where He is with all of our hearts.

As we watched our televisions on that fateful day of 9/11, we saw people who were desperately calling on God in their time of need . . . and the stories of the miracles that occurred on that day confirms to us that God did keep His promise in His word that says: "Call on me and I will answer you" (Jer. 33:3). The victims of 9/11 called upon God in their time of desperation and earnestness. It is this degree of earnestness that God wants us to have when we seek Him.

In the Greek text, the word "face" translates to the phrase "His presence." God desires that when we seek His presence, we are to meet Him "face to face" . . . and the term "face to face" in terms of closeness also translates into the words "mouth to mouth." God desires us to be so close to Him that if we could, we would be able to touch His nose with our nose, His mouth with our mouth, and gaze into His eyes! In terms of closeness, God is talking about you and I being closer to Him "than a brother" (Prov. 18:24). Loving God with all of your heart, soul, mind, and strength means that you should be in the continual state of seeking God in earnest.

". . . and I will heal their land."

The word "heal in both the Old and New Testament meant "to make whole, or to save." To receive healing from God is to receive abundant deliverance. The word "heal" has a direct relationship to the word "escape" in the Bible. So when God promises "I will heal their land," it does not simply refer to wellness or exemption from disease. It also means deliverance from affliction or trial or catastrophe.

When King David conquered all of the enemies that were surrounding Israel, it was said that all of David's enemies knew "That there was a God in Israel." Why? Because there was abundant proof that the God of Abraham, Isaac and Jacob was actively working to fight David's battles for him. God was in the act of "abundant deliverance," and that is the meaning of God's other promise in 2 Chron. 7:14 "I will heal their land."

There is no doubt that this very same condition of "abundant deliverance" was at work in Colonial America. For example, for Washington to have been shot at repeatedly at the Battle of the Monongahela in 1755 and emerge unscathed was surely an act of God's providence and protection. For the Continental Army to have spent such a desperate winter at Valley Forge and then be reinforced and refitted by Lafayette was truly a providential occurrence. Only a sincere, heart-felt turning towards God by the American people at that time could have brought the divine deliverance of healing on the American colonies in their most desperate hour.

And so it can be with us . . . the movement of our people once again to a dual covenant relationship with God and our people can bring about the healing of our nation. Where did the people of the

Massachusett's Bay Colony get their inspiration in writing the Mayflower Compact and developing the dual contract between God and their fellow colonists? They did not have to look far . . . for they found the blueprint of the dual covenant in Christ's Great Commandment in Matthew 22:37–39: "Love the Lord your God with all of your heart, soul, mind and strength . . . and love your neighbor as yourself."

Most Christians are convinced that by resolving to treat all of their brothers and sisters in Christ equally, they have fulfilled the second part of the Great Commandment. But again, if the true meaning of the love of Christ, Agape love, is interpreted properly, the commitment to serve others based on that love would not be so lightly given. For Christ's love always begins with the bowl and towel . . . the willingness to do the un-lovely task for others. And the depth of that same agape love of Christ ends with His sacrifice of the cross. So the true meaning of the Mayflower covenant was that the pilgrims pledged to serve each other with the agape love of Christ to the extent that they were willing to sacrifice themselves for others. This was a powerful and dynamic commitment on the part of the pilgrims . . . for without this total effort of serving and helping each other, they would have all perished.

But what has changed today in terms of what is required from God's people? Without unity, without the desire to serve and share with one another unconditionally, the reason for our very existence and mission on this earth is lost! Serving God and serving their fellow man . . . that has always been God's plan for His people.

CHAPTER NINE

The Solution

$\mathcal{E}$veryone knows the motto of the U.S. Marines: "We need a few good men!" The United States Marines are the smallest branch of the four major services branches in the armed forces, but they are the most distinguished and well-respected of the four. Why? Because they have based their success on the principle that a small number of well-armed and well-trained men, combined with the element of surprise, can make a huge difference in any armed conflict. And it is the same with God's promise to us in 2 Chronicles 7:14. "If my people" does not refer to everyone, rather it refers only to those who are willing to stand in the gap and intercede for our people and our nation in God's presence. Our Lord Jesus chose only twelve disciples. He did not need thousands or even hundreds to spread His gospel around the world. Twelve disciples were enough to catalyze a great Christian movement, marked by the birth of Christ's church in the first century A.D.

The solution to our nation's problems is the same solution that God has responded to with those who are obedient to Him throughout history. The solution is that we must begin to pray . . . pray with a few dedicated brothers and sisters that are as committed as you are to stand in the gap and intercede for our nation.

But remember! Your approach to this intercessory prayer is going to be very different from anything that you have attempted in all of your Christian walk. Realize that in your intercession, you are seeking the same two-pronged relationship between God and man that your forefathers sought so many years ago. The pilgrims covenanted with God first, that they as individuals and as a people would remain obedient and faithful to Him, seeking His direction and guidance in their daily lives. Secondly, the pilgrims pledged to remain in a covenant relationship with their fellow believers, to honor and to serve each other in Agape love, the love practiced by Jesus Christ. Their goal was to become as one body under God, similar to the Christian church of the first century A.D.

The book of Acts in the Bible is proof to us that the first century church was a product of this dual covenant between God and man. Acts 2:42 says that the church "devoted itself to prayer" and "every day they met together, praising God" (v. 46). These early church members were first focused on listening to and obeying God. Then, verse 44 says, "all the believers were together and had everything in common." They served their fellow man with the very love of their master, Jesus Christ. The early church based their dual covenant on the same Great Commandment that Jesus gave His disciples in Matt. 22:37–39 and it was no coincidence that our pilgrim forefathers did the very same thing in the Mayflower Compact. It is interesting to note that the Virginia Colony in Roanoke was a completely secular colony, with no clergy or spiritual leadership, and no families . . . simply a colony of adult males. Without the reality of God to sustain them in their time of need, the Virginia colony failed, while the Massachusett's Bay Colony survived.

Sadly, when communicating with Americans, both secular and Christian, on the subject of America's Christian heritage, it is the Christian populace that seems to be the most skeptical concerning that subject. Why is this so? Why would Christians have a hard time believing that America was founded upon Christian principles? Perhaps it is the fact that we are presently a secular nation . . . and that bothers the Christian skeptics. Their belief is that if we were truly once a great Christian nation, then we should still be one today if God had truly had His hand in the creation of this country. But the fact is that our Christian history is recorded and preserved in every library and bookstore across this nation in some form or fashion . . . and the proof of our history is there for the asking, if we would just make the effort to discover it.

So we have discovered that the spiritual blessings of America began with the Mayflower Compact, the covenant created by the Massachusetts Bay Colony. And that document was based on Christ's Great Commandment found in Matt. 22:37–39 of the Bible. Then, it stands to reason that the successful prayer for spiritual renewal in America should be based on the same dual covenant with God and our fellow man. Our prayer to that effect should sound something like this: "Lord, I turn my life over to you in humility and obedience . . . help me to follow You in faith with all of my heart. Lord, help me also to serve my fellow man with the same love that your son, Jesus, taught us to serve with . . . the love that is based on His sacrifice for us on the cross."

This must be our prayer. For the realization of this dual relationship with God and our fellow man requires the constant seeking of the ear of God. And if we seek to live a life based on this dual covenant diligently, with all of our hearts, then God will restore this nation back to the spiritual and material place of refuge to the world that it once was.

So, covenant to pray with a few faithful prayer warriors in a small group to start with. Then, expand your prayer sessions to include other members of your church and friendship circle. And simultaneously, your prayer life must begin to correspond with your life of service to others. In your prayers, ask God who you might serve and how you might serve them. Because this service to others is based on the Agape love of Jesus Christ, then your service to others must be sacrificial and unconditional. We must link our prayer for revival to a lifestyle of sacrificial service. Remember that history tells us that our pilgrim forefathers began this dual covenant process with just a few friends. Many others in the Mayflower party were not Christians, but they eventually discovered the great value in such a covenant, and they asked to join in . . . and they eventually became Christians! So do not be surprised if the same thing happens in your small group. Once people learn that you are re-creating history by imitating our pilgrim forefathers in this dual covenant between God and man, others may want to participate simply because of the historic value or the uniqueness of the approach. But whatever the reason that people participate in this prayer process,

God will do mighty things through your efforts. God has always done great things through the small groups of people that the world has considered "inadequate" or "not qualified." The path back to the Christian values of our past must begin somewhere . . . so let it begin with you, in your heart!

Prologue

*I*mmediately following the 9/11 disaster, the news media began to interview anyone and everyone of any significance who had an opinion on the event. The media finally cornered Anne Graham Lotz, noted author, evangelist, and daughter of the evangelist Billy Graham. A reporter asked Ms. Lotz: "How could God allow something like this to happen to us?" Ms. Lotz' answer should be recorded in our nation's history as one of the most significant statements ever made during a time of national tragedy. She said:

"We have asked God to leave every public institution and walk of life here in America. Our schools, our workplaces, our government and

legal system . . . and you ask: 'Why did God allow this to happen?' It happened because we
have told God that we no longer need Him!
There is no doubt in my mind that had we not
rejected God, the tragedy of 9/11 never would
have happened."

No greater truth was spoken by anyone in the
days and weeks after the World Trade Center disaster . . . but sadly, what Ms. Lotz said went largely
unnoticed. And sadder still, nothing has changed
since 9/11. We are still a secular nation that gives
homage to the Creator only when it is convenient
to our busy schedules. The true lessons of our
nation's history have yet to be rediscovered by the
descendants of the Founding Fathers . . . and that
is, God will provide for and protect those who love,
honor and obey Him. And to those that turn their
backs on God, nothing but tragedy and suffering
await those who do. James 4:6 says "God opposes
the proud, but gives grace to the humble." Galatians
6:7 says "Do not be deceived, God cannot be
mocked. A man will reap what he sows." If we ig-
nore God as a nation, we will reap the harvest of
that neglect, just as we did on September 11th.

2 Chronicles 7:14

Conclusion

$\mathcal{I}$ have come to the conclusion that the Great Commandment of Jesus found in Mark 12:30 calls every follower of Jesus Christ to a covenant relationship between God and his fellow men. I also believe that the lack of covenanting the Great Commandment is what has been lacking in all of the calls to revival during the 20th century in America. The key to beginning a covenant relationship with both God and man can be found in the small group setting. The most dynamic and compelling book on this subject of covenant relationship is the book: "Cultivating a Life for God" by Neil Cole*. I urge you to form covenant relationships with a few of

---

*Church Smart Resources, Publishers, ISBN #1-889638-06-4

your closest fellow believers, and then multiply the covenant relationship by forming new groups with your original members as group leaders. Remember that Valley Forge was called: "The Crucible of Freedom" because Washington was calling his men into covenant relationship between God and their fellow soldiers. I urge you to read Mr. Cole's book and begin to initiate covenant relationship between God, you and your fellow believers.

May God bless you!!

JDM

Endnotes

Chapter One

    1. Barton, David, "America's Godly Heritage," video tape, section 2, unit 2, Wallbuilder Press, Copy. 1992

Chapter Two

    1. Combee, Dr. Jerry H., "History of the World in Christian Perspective," Abeka Pub., Copy. 1992, ppg. 187–188
    2. Ibid, ppg. 212–214
    3. Marshall, Peter, "The Light and the Glory," Fleming-Revell Publishers, Copy. 1977, ppg. 248–249

4. Duewel, Wesley, "Revival Fire," Zondervan Publishing Co., Copy. 1995, ppg. 59–61

Chapter Three

1. Barton, David, "America's Godly Heritage," Video, Wallbuilder Press, Copy. 1992, section 1, part 3
2. Various Authors, "America—Great Crises in our History Told by its Makers," Vol. 4, V.F.W. Pub., Copy. 1923, ppg. 209–223
3. Barton, David, "America's Godly Heritage," video tape, Wallbuilder Press, Copy. 1992, section 3, part 3
4. Ibid, section 3, part 4
5. Ibid, section 1, part 2
6. Ibid, section 1, part 3

Chapter Four

1. Combee, Dr. Jerry H., "The History of the World in Christian Perspective, Abeka Pub., Copy. 1995, ppg. 157–160
2. Marshall, Peter, "The Light and the Glory," Fleming-Revell Publishers, Copy. 1977, Thomas Paine's "Common Sense," ppg. 97–102
3. Ibid, Columbus' diaries, ppg. 17–18
4. Ibid, Columbus' diaries, ppg. 31–39

5. Ibid, Cotton Mather, ppg. 176–178
6. Various Authors, "America—Great Crises in our History Told by its Makers, V.F.W. Press, Copy. 1923, Vol 3-Revolution, ppg. 106–114
7. Marshall, Peter, "The Light and the Glory," Fleming-Revell Pubishers, Copy. 1977, ppg. 284–5

Chapter Five

1. Barton, David, "America's Godly Heritage," video tape, Wallbuilder Press, Copy. 1992, section 2, part 1
2. Ibid, section 2, part 2
3. Marshall, Peter, "The Light and the Glory," Fleming-Revell Publishers, Copy. 1977, pg. 344

Chapter Six

1. Barton, David, "America's Godly Heritage," video tape, Wallbuilder Press, Copy. 1992, section 2, part 1
2. Ibid, section 3, part 2
3. Ibid, section 3, part 3
4. Ibid, section 3, part 1

Chapter Seven

1. Abraham, Henry, "Justices and Presidents— A History of the Appointments to the Supreme Court," Harper and Rowe Pub., Copy. 1963, ppg. 126–135
2. Ibid, ppg. 203
3. Ibid, ppg. 211–214

Chapter Eight

1. Millard, Catherine, "Great American Statesmen and Heroes," Horizon Publishers, Copy. 1995, ppg. 295–296
2. Marshall, Peter, "The Light and the Glory," Fleming-Revell Publishers, Copy. 1977, ppg. 355–360

Bibliography

Abraham, Henry, "Justices and Presidents—A History of Appointments to the Supreme Court," Harper and Rowe, Publishers, Copy. 1963

Cobb, Sanford H., "The Rise of Religious Liberty in America," McMillan and Co. New York, Copy. 1902

Combee, Dr. Henry H., "The History of the World in a Christian Perspective," Abeka Publishing, Copy. 1961

Duewel, Wesley, "Revival Fire," Zondervan Publishing Co. Grand Rapids, Mich. Copy. 1995

Edwards, Jonathan, "Thoughts on the Revival of Religion in New England," published by

The American Tract Society, New York, Copy. 1740

Hall, Verna M., "The Christian History of the American Revolution," Foundation for American Christian Education, San Francisco, Copy. 1976

Heimert, Alan, "Religion and the American Mind," Harvard University Press Publishers, Cambridge, Mass. Copy. 1966

Johnson, William J., "George Washington the Christian," Abington Press, Nashville, Tenn. Copy. 1919

Keller, Charles R., "The Second Great Awakening," Yale University Press, New Haven, Conn. Copy. 1942

Lancaster, Bruce, "The American Heritage Book of the Revolution," Dell Publishing Co. New York, Copy. 1958

Marty, Martin E., "The Protestant Experience in America," Dial Press, New York, Copy. 1970

Mead, Sidney E., "The Shaping of Christianity in America," Harper and Rowe, New York, 1963

Niebuhr, Richard, "The Kingdom of God in America," Harper and Rowe, New York, Copy. 1959

Microsoft Encarta Encyclopedia, Pub 1993, Microsoft Corp., "The Great Awakening" Pages 1–2

Millard, Catherine, "Great American Statesmen and Heroes," Horizon Publishing, Camp Hill, Pa. Copy. 1995

Peters, John L., "Christian Perfection and American Methodism," Asbury Press, Copy. 1956

Padover, Saul K., "Jefferson—A Great American's Life and Ideas," Mentor Publishing, Copy. 1942

Smith, Tim L., "The Pentecostal Hymns of John and Charles Wesley," Beacon Hill Press, Copy. 1982

Wesley, John, "My Personal Journal," Percy L. Parker, Editor, Moody Press, Chicago, Copy. 1974

Wiltse, Charles M., "The Jeffersonian Tradition in American Democracy," Hill and Wang Publishers, Copy. 1935

To order additional copies of

THE
PEARL
OF GREAT
PRICE

Have your credit card ready and call:

1-877-421-READ (7323)

or please visit our web site at
www.pleasantword.com

Also available at: www.amazon.com

Printed in the United States
203269BV00006B/4/A

9 781414 100807